THE **FUTURE** OF **POWER**

HARNESSING
HYDROELECTRIC
ENERGY

NANCY DICKMANN

PowerKiDS
press.

NEW YORK

Published in 2017 by
The Rosen Publishing Group, Inc.
29 East 21st Street, New York, NY 10010

Cataloging-in-Publication Data

Names: Dickmann, Nancy.
Title: Harnessing hydroelectric energy / Nancy Dickmann.
Description: New York : PowerKids Press, 2017. | Series: The future of power | Includes index.
Identifiers: ISBN 9781499432121 (pbk.) | ISBN 9781499432312 (library bound) |
  ISBN 9781508153306 (6 pack)
Subjects: LCSH: Hydroelectric power plants--Juvenile literature.
Classification: LCC TK1081.D54 2017 | DDC 621.31'2134--dc23

For Brown Bear Books Ltd:
Editor: Tim Harris
Editorial Director: Lindsey Lowe
Children's Publisher: Anne O'Daly
Design Manager: Keith Davis
Picture Manager: Sophie Mortimer

Picture Credits: t=top, c=center, b=bottom, l=left, r=right. Interior: 123rf: 21t; Library of
Congress: 15t; Public Domain: EEP 17t; Shutterstock: 5, 6, 7, 13, 21b, 24, 27, 28, Ralf Broskvar 15,
Claude Hunt 22, Skylight Pictures 10, David Taljat 25; US Army: Corps of Engineers 12, 18-19;
Wikipedia: 9, Matt Ragen 29, Sirbatch 17b .

Manufactured in the United States of America
CPSIA Compliance Information: Batch #BW17RK: For Further Information contact Rosen Publishing, New York, New York at 1-800-237-9932

CONTENTS

RIVER POWER

When a river goes over a cliff, immense amounts of water cascade down to form a waterfall. The water ends up far below, where the river continues, sending clouds of mist billowing into the air. The movement of the river's water gives it a type of energy called kinetic energy.

Any object in motion has kinetic energy. Large rivers carry huge amounts of water, giving them a lot of kinetic energy. For centuries people have used the energy of moving water to power mills. Flowing water turns a waterwheel, which then rotates a millstone. The turning millstone grinds grain into flour.

ENERGY NEEDS

Today, our energy needs are more complex. We depend on electricity to power a huge range of tools—from electric toothbrushes to factory machinery. There are many ways of generating electricity. Some involve burning fuels such as coal, oil, or natural gas. But we can also harness the kinetic energy of moving water to run our power plants. Instead of spinning a waterwheel, a river's water can spin turbines that generate electricity for us to use.

THIS OLD WATERWHEEL IS IN ITALY. WATER TURNS THE WHEEL, AND THE WHEEL TURNS A MILLSTONE, WHICH GRINDS GRAIN.

Rivers flow downhill because of the force of gravity, which pulls everything on Earth toward Earth's center. A river has its source at high altitude, and gravity pulls the water downhill to lower elevations—and eventually into the sea. Rivers always flow downhill, though in some places their course is steeper than in others.

Rivers are part of a system known as the water cycle, in which the water moves from one place to another. As the Sun heats Earth, water at the surface evaporates and turns into water vapor. The water vapor rises into the air, forming clouds. Eventually, the clouds release the water as rain or snow. This falls to Earth, often ending up in rivers or streams. The water cycle ensures that rivers have a constant supply of flowing water.

WATER CYCLE

The amount of water on Earth is more or less constant. The same molecules of water are constantly moving around as part of the water cycle, getting recycled over and over. In fact, the water molecules you drink today may have once been drunk by a dinosaur, millions of years ago.

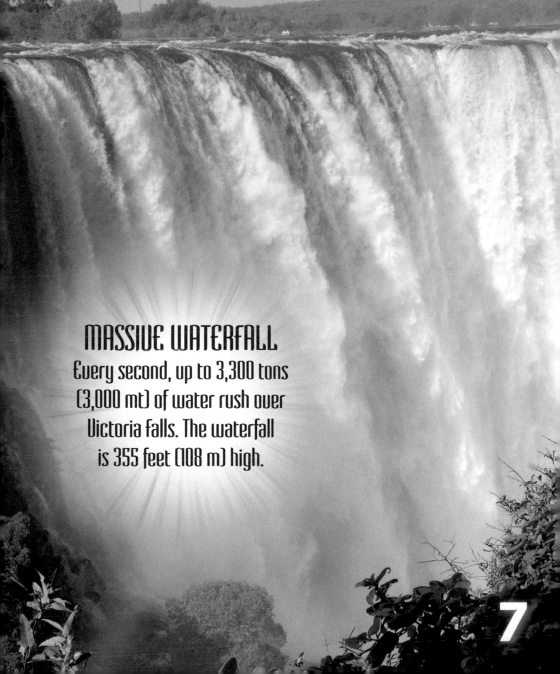

MASSIVE WATERFALL

Every second, up to 3,300 tons (3,000 mt) of water rush over Victoria falls. The waterfall is 355 feet (108 m) high.

HOW DOES IT WORK?

In ancient times, people used the energy of rivers to turn grain mills or sawmills, or to pump water for irrigating crops. But in the 18th century, factory owners realized that they could use this energy to power their heavy machinery. In England, waterwheels provided the power to keep textile mills working.

The use of rivers to generate electricity is more recent. In 1827, the French engineer Benoit Fourneyron invented a turbine that was much more efficient than old-style waterwheels. In the decades that followed, other engineers developed even better turbines. The first use of hydropower to generate electricity took place in 1878 at Cragside, a house in England where a small device called a dynamo powered an electric light.

THE FIRST HYDRO PLANTS

Just four years later, in 1882, a hydroelectric plant was opened in Appleton, Wisconsin. The waters of the Fox River spun a turbine that generated enough electricity to light two paper mills and a house. Within a decade, dozens more hydroelectric plants had opened around the world.

ONE OF THE FIRST

The Uzice hydroelectric plant is one of the oldest in the world. It began to produce electricity in 1900 and powered a textile factory, as well as lighting all the houses in the town.

THE FIRST HYDROPLANT BUILT IN THE BALKAN MOUNTAINS IS AT UZICE, ON THE DJETINJA RIVER IN SERBIA.

9

BIG WORKS BEST

The bigger the amount of water flowing past a turbine, and the faster it moves, the more electricity it can generate. Engineers realized that building large dams was a good way of increasing the amount of electricity they could produce.

By building a dam across a river, a huge amount of water could be held back in a reservoir. Electricity is hard to store, but the water behind a dam could be released to flow through the turbines only when it was needed. This gave engineers the control to produce more electricity during times of peak demand.

In the 20th century, enormous dams were built in many locations. Construction started on the Grand Coulee Dam in Washington State in 1933. The Boulder Dam, on the border of Nevada and Arizona, opened in 1936. Its name was later changed to the Hoover Dam. Huge projects like these used natural resources to provide electricity on a grand scale.

By 1949, almost one-third of the electricity in the United States came from hydropower, and other countries used it, too. The Itaipu Dam in South America opened in 1984. It was the largest hydroelectric plant in the world until the Three Gorges Dam in China surpassed it.

BUILDING A DAM

Building a dam in a flowing river is not an easy job. To make a dry area for construction, engineers dump gravel into the river to form a temporary barrier, or cofferdam. This encloses an area of the river. The water is pumped out, providing a dry place to start building the dam. Once one section is finished, the cofferdam is removed and the next section is built.

The faster water falls, the more energy it has, so a river with a large drop in elevation is a good place for a hydroelectric dam. Dams are often built at a point where a river narrows. Engineers must make sure that the surrounding landscape is strong enough to bear the enormous weight of the dam itself, and of the water stored in the reservoir.

There are different kinds of dams. A gravity dam such as the Itaipu Dam is a massive structure built of concrete or stone, which uses its own weight to stop the flow of the river. An arch dam, such as the Hoover Dam, is thinner but has a stronger, curved shape to stop the water. Arch dams are often built in narrow canyons.

THIS ARCH DAM AT KAPRUN IN AUSTRIA (BELOW) HOLDS BACK A DEEP RESERVOIR. THERE IS A HYDROPLANT INSIDE THE DAM.

BIGGEST ARCH DAM

The world's biggest arch dam is at Jinping on the Yalong River in China. It is 1,000 feet (305 m) tall.

13

HOW A DAM WORKS

No matter what the dam looks like, the basic setup for a hydroelectric power station is the same. The water stored in the reservoir has potential energy. This potential energy is converted to kinetic energy when the water starts moving through the dam. The dam has an opening on the reservoir side, called the intake, and it has sluice gates that can be opened or closed to control the flow of water.

When the gates are open, gravity forces water into a pipeline called the penstock, which runs through the dam. The pressure of the water increases as it flows downward through the penstock. There is a turbine at the end of the penstock, and the force of the moving water makes the turbine spin. A large dam can have more than a dozen enormous turbines.

The spinning turbine's shaft is connected to a generator, which has powerful magnets that can turn kinetic energy into an electric current. The electricity flows out of the power plant along wires that take it wherever it is needed. After it has gone through the turbine, the water flows along through an outflow pipe (called a tailrace) and back into the river, to continue its journey to the sea.

TURBINE SHAFT

These workers are installing the steel shaft that connects a turbine and an electricity generator in a hydroelectric power station. When water turns the turbine, the shaft spins the generator.

SOME OF THE GENERATORS AT THE HOOVER DAM ON THE COLORADO RIVER. WHEN FIRST BUILT, THIS WAS THE WORLD'S BIGGEST HYDROPLANT.

PUMPED STORAGE PLANT

In a conventional hydroelectric plant, the water is only used once before it flows downstream. But in a pumped-storage plant, there is a second reservoir below the dam. After water flows through the turbines, it goes into the lower reservoir. During times when there is less demand for electricity—for example, in the middle of the night—water is pumped back up to the upper reservoir. This means that it can flow back through to generate more electricity at times of peak demand.

You can even generate hydroelectric power without a reservoir! A run-of-the-river system generates electricity while still allowing the river to flow naturally. It works by diverting part or all of a river's flow to a penstock that leads through a turbine, then back into the river. However, since there is no storage, the amount and the timing of the electricity produced is difficult to control.

"THE BIGGEST BATTERY"

The world's biggest pumped-storage plant is in Bath County, Virginia. It has been described as "the biggest battery in the world" and can generate 3,000 megawatts of electricity.

MINI-HYDRO

Some hydroelectric power plants are very small. "Pico hydro" is a term used to describe setups making less than 1 megawatt of electricity. They can only power a few homes but are very useful in remote locations, where there is no grid electricity.

THE CASTAIC PUMPED-STORAGE PLANT IN CALIFORNIA SUPPLIES LOS ANGELES WITH ELECTRICITY.

GOOD AND BAD

Only some of our electricity is generated from hydroelectric power. Other power plants use steam instead of running water to spin turbines and generate electricity. The heat needed to turn water into steam comes from burning coal, oil, and natural gas. These are called fossil fuels.

Fossil fuels are found deep underground, and they are not renewable. This means that once we have extracted Earth's supply of them, there will be no more. On the other hand, hydroelectric

FOSSIL FUELS RUNNING OUT

The three fossil fuels—oil, natural gas, and coal—were formed millions of years ago when dead plants and animals were buried and compressed. They created carbon-rich sources of fuel which will run out eventually.

18

power is renewable. Thanks to the water cycle, our supply of moving water will never run out.

Hydroelectricity has another advantage over fossil fuels: it's a cleaner form of energy. Fossil fuels release gases into the atmosphere when they burn, causing pollution as well as global warming. Some pollution is created when a dam is built, but once it is up and running, the electricity it generates is very clean.

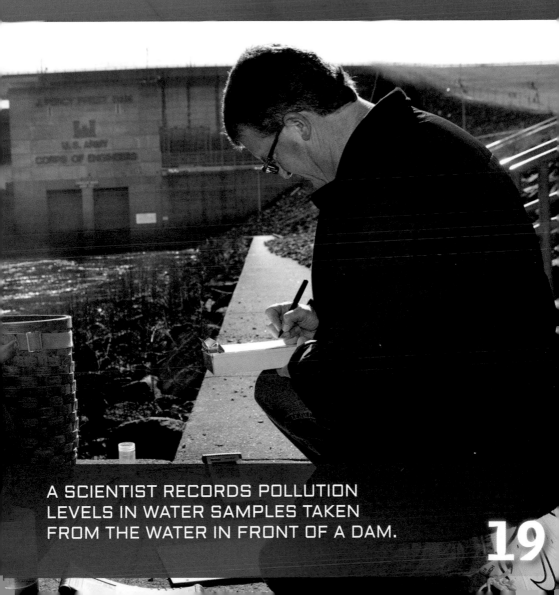

A SCIENTIST RECORDS POLLUTION
LEVELS IN WATER SAMPLES TAKEN
FROM THE WATER IN FRONT OF A DAM.

One of the main benefits of hydropower is its flexibility. A moving river provides a constant and reliable source of power, day and night. Building a dam allows engineers to control the flow, so that more electricity can be generated when it is needed, and less at times of lower demand.

Hydropower is also flexible in terms of scale. Large dams can supply electricity to millions of people, but much smaller hydroelectric plants can power smaller towns or villages—or even a single building. It is useful in areas where there are no other reliable sources of electricity.

Compared to other forms of renewable energy, such as wind and solar power, hydroelectricity is fairly cheap. The cost of building a dam can be huge, but once it is up and running, the maintenance and operation costs are low. However, in many places it is still more expensive than burning coal and other fossil fuels.

DRINKING WATER

River water builds up behind dams to form reservoirs. These can supply water for drinking and for irrigation. Lake Mead, which formed behind the Hoover Dam, provides water for 20 million people.

ELECTRICITY GRID

Electricity from a hydroelectric power station is carried by wires and pylons to the grid system.

WHEN FULL OF WATER, LAKE MEAD IS 112 MILES (180 KM) LONG AND 562 FEET (162 M) DEEP.

HOOVER DAM HOLDS BACK LAKE MEAD. A DROUGHT HAS REDUCED THE AMOUNT OF WATER FLOWING INTO THE LAKE, SO THERE IS LESS WATER TO DRIVE THE DAM'S TURBINES.

DROUGHT AND EXPENSE

Hydroelectric power is far from perfect. While this power is generally reliable, a drought reduces the volume of water flowing in a river. The river may even dry up completely, and this will affect the electricity supply.

Some countries use hydroelectricity to generate a large percentage of their electricity, while other countries hardly use it at all. One reason for this is cost. Building a large dam is a huge, expensive job, but it must be done at the start, before an energy company can start making money by selling electricity. In many countries, the initial investment needed is just too high to afford.

SUITABLE LOCATIONS

In addition, dams can't be built just anywhere. Large hydroelectric plants only work in locations where there is a big river with a large drop in elevation. Flatter countries, such as the Netherlands, don't have many of these locations. Many of the best locations for large dams around the world are already being used.

Small-scale hydroelectric and run-of-the river systems can work in locations that aren't suitable for big dams. They are also cheaper to build, but they produce much less electricity.

Some dams block a river completely, making it impossible for ships and fish to get past. People have solved this problem by building locks, which ships can move through. Some dams have fish ladders, where fish swim or leap up a series of steps to cross the dam.

A river is an ecosystem, and building a dam can upset it. Creating a reservoir usually means flooding the land around a river, which can include forests, farmers' fields, and towns. More than 1 million people had to leave their homes when the Three Gorges Dam was built across the Yangtze River in China. The reservoir behind the dam later flooded their homes.

Dams can affect water levels. Water evaporates more quickly from a reservoir than from a flowing river. If the dam doesn't let enough water through, parts of the river farther downstream may dry out.

RIVER DOLPHINS

Freshwater dolphins once swam in China's Yangtze River. They may now be extinct. Scientists think that a mixture of shipping and dams across the Yangtze River damaged the dolphins' habitat too much for them to survive.

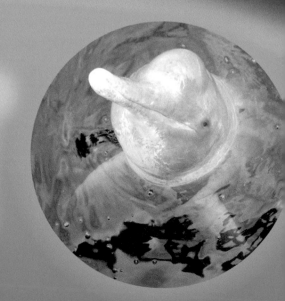

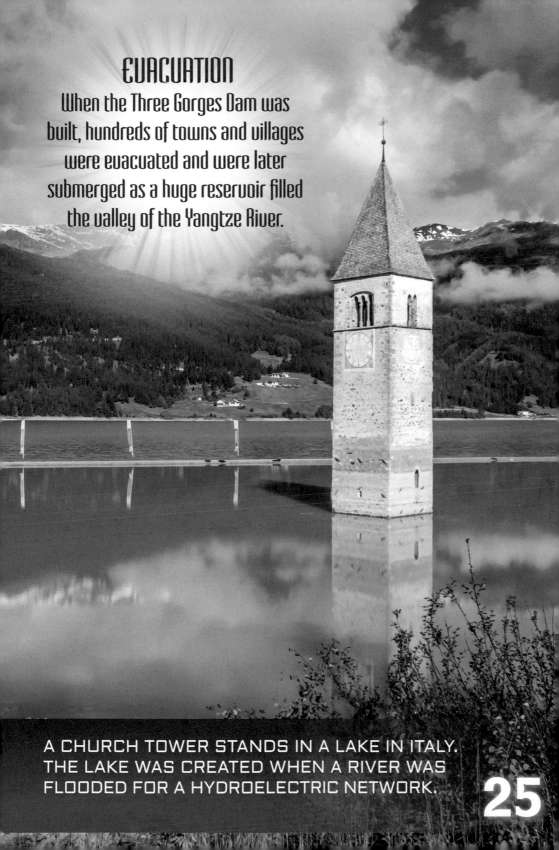

EVACUATION

When the Three Gorges Dam was built, hundreds of towns and villages were evacuated and were later submerged as a huge reservoir filled the valley of the Yangtze River.

A CHURCH TOWER STANDS IN A LAKE IN ITALY. THE LAKE WAS CREATED WHEN A RIVER WAS FLOODED FOR A HYDROELECTRIC NETWORK.

25

THE FUTURE

Because we need to reduce our dependence on fossil fuels, renewable energy is becoming more important. Hydropower is currently the source of about 16 percent of the world's electricity, making it the most widely used source of renewable energy.

More than 150 countries use hydropower to supply at least part of their energy needs. In the United States, hydropower only makes up about 6 percent of total electricity, but in other countries it is much higher: about 60 percent in Canada, 75 percent in Brazil, and nearly 100 percent in Mozambique.

Some scientists believe that if we build power stations in the right places, Earth's rivers could provide four times as much electricity as they currently generate. Many of the most promising locations are in developing countries.

ACTUAL AND POTENTIAL

China, Brazil, Canada, and the United States generate more electricity from hydroelectric networks than any other countries. Even so, scientists believe China could produce ten times more hydroelectricity than it does.

THE YARLUNG ZANGBO RIVER IN TIBET FLOWS
THROUGH THE WORLD'S LARGEST CANYON.
THIS VALLEY WOULD BE AN IDEAL PLACE FOR
A HYDROELECTRIC NETWORK.

Using renewable energy, such as hydroelectricity, can help fight climate change, but climate change is already having an impact on hydroelectric networks. In many places, changing weather patterns are bringing long droughts. Lower water levels in rivers mean that less electricity can be generated. For example, California's hydroelectricity production was cut in half during a recent drought, when less water was flowing in rivers.

Warmer average temperatures are causing glaciers to melt. This means that in the future there may be less water flowing through many of Earth's rivers. Engineers are redesigning turbines and dams to make them more efficient, even with lower water levels. A recent project at Hoover Dam overhauled its turbines to make them produce more electricity.

NEW IDEAS

Scientists are also looking for new ways to generate electricity from moving water. There are pipes beneath our feet with water flowing through them—either bringing clean water to our faucets, or taking wastewater away. Small turbines in these pipes can generate electricity as the water moves. This means that every time you flush a toilet or take a shower, you generate electricity! Innovations like these could mean that we get even more of our energy from hydropower in the future.

GLOSSARY

dynamo: A machine that produces electricity.

ecosystem: A community of plants and animals that interact with each other and their environment.

generator: A device that turns mechanical energy into electricity.

glacier: A large area of thick ice that remains frozen from one year to the next.

global warming: An increase in the average temperature of Earth's atmosphere.

grid: A power transmission network taking electricity from where it is generated to where it is needed.

megawatt (MW): A large unit of electricity. One MW can provide all the electricity for more than several hundred houses.

molecules: The smallest units of a substance that have all the properties of that substance. Air is made up mostly of molecules of nitrogen and oxygen.

pollution: The release of substances that have harmful or toxic effects into the atmosphere, rivers, or ocean.

reservoir: An artificial lake held back by a dam.

shaft: A bar in a machine that turns other parts that move or spin.

turbine: A machine with blades attached to a central rotating shaft. Turbines are used to generate electricity.

FURTHER INFORMATION

BOOKS

Bailey, Dianne. *Hydropower* (Harnessing Energy). West Mankato, MA: Creative, 2015.

Challoner, Jack. *Energy* (Eyewitness). New York: Dorling Kindersley, 2012.

Rodger, Marguerite. *Hydroelecric Power: Power from Moving Water* (Energy Revolution). New York: Crabtree, 2010.

WEBSITES

Due to the changing nature of Internet links, PowerKids Press has developed an online list of websites related to the subject of this book. This site is updated regularly. Please use this link to access the list:

www.powerkidslinks.com/tfon/hydro

INDEX